The Future
for
Baby Boomers
(As I See It)

The Future for Baby Boomers
(As I See It)

By
David Leber

E-BookTime, LLC
Montgomery, Alabama

The Future for Baby Boomers
(As I See It)

Copyright © 2006 by David Leber

Library of Congress Control Number: 2006936647

ISBN: 1-59824-324-1

First Edition
Published October 2006
E-BookTime, LLC
6598 Pumpkin Road
Montgomery, AL 36108
www.e-booktime.com

Contents

Contents

Introduction

As I write this book just before my 60th birthday, I realize that the future for baby boomers is very important. There are about 78 million of us in the United States alone, and I am fortunate to be one of the early boomers, having been born in 1946. I feel that I've had some fairly significant experiences in my almost 60 years, having been a psychology major at the University of Pennsylvania and focusing on the study of human behavior and motivation.

For over 37 years, I've been a financial, business and lifestyle advisor, mostly to our own baby boomer generation. As a Certified Financial Planner®, Chartered Financial Consultant and Certified Senior Advisor, I have worked with hundreds of businesses and families helping them to chart the territory to financial independence.

During that time, I've continued to be a significant student of motivation and human behavior. My first book, *Finding Your True Self*, was created in 1996 and was designed to be a guide for self-awareness and self-actualization. My second book, *Taking Charge: Life Enhancing Strategies for People Over 40*, written in 2001, was designed to be a combination of financial and lifestyle guidelines for people in their 40s, 50s, 60s and even beyond. My third work, *Giving Back: Making Life Better for Ourselves and Our Society*, was created in 2003 and was intended to cover the importance of philanthropy and volunteerism and the importance of helping others less fortunate than ourselves.

Frankly, I thought I was finished with writing books after *Giving Back* was published. However, in March of 2006, while vacationing in the French West Indies, my good friend, Dr. Karlene ChinQuee, inspired me to write another book. The ideas immediately came to me, and I outlined the chapters and the idea for the book. I committed to Karlene to have the book finished by my 60th birthday, and here it is! (By the way, proceeds from this book will go to Karlene's foundation, Heartbeats of the World, Inc., which helps young girls in

Jamaica and other underdeveloped countries avoid pregnancy and poverty and learn to work in the hospitality trades.)

I hope you find at least one or two good ideas in this book. My purpose in all of the books I've created is to cover the basics and the fundamentals in an easily readable format so that you can cover the material in an hour or so. It's also designed to be read and reviewed more than once and the text to be underlined and highlighted. My goal in a book like this is not to cover everything you need to know, but to give you at least one or two good ideas that make sense and that you can put into practice. I realize I've covered a lot of fundamentals of which you're already aware, but I hope I've covered some new areas for you, as well. I'd also be interested in your responses and feedback to the book if you have any. Feel free to contact me at dave@leberfinancial.com. I'd especially like to thank my administrative assistant, Sharon Kuzma, who helped me put the book together.

Chapter 1

What to Expect
(As If Anyone Really Knows)

We baby boomers (I turned 60 in July 2006) are being bombarded with statistics and projections regarding what our generation can expect in the future. The truth is that none of us is the same, and we can't all be put into categories. However, we baby boomers do have a lot in common. Many of us will not be able to "retire" in the traditional sense. So what, I say. The paradigm of traditional retirement has already changed over the past 10 to 15 years. Some of us, the lucky and talented top 3 percent to 5 percent financially, will be able to stop working completely if we choose to in our 50s or 60s and continue to enjoy the lifestyle we've come to expect. The other 95 percent or so will be faced with important decisions—either continue working beyond normal retirement ages of 60 to 65, or adjust our lifestyles downward. Many baby boomers already don't enjoy their current lifestyle and may be forced to cut back even more.

My response is that we have choices—we can accept this fate, or take steps to change it by continuing to work in some capacity, even in a different type of work, or in a scaled-back capacity. We also may have to be concerned about Social Security, a possible healthcare crisis and long-term care needs as we get older. While these are legitimate concerns, I don't think we should be consumed by worry and run the risk of our status getting even worse. Instead, we need to be aware of these risks and be ready to make changes if we have to. Our generation certainly has been exposed to change and the need to be adaptable. I say let's look forward to the future with positive expectations and not trepidation. Let's plan for the future to some degree, but balance our current needs and wants with some protection for the future; if things work out as we hope, all the better. But if they don't, then let's be prepared to make adjustments. We can have a nice future in either event by adjusting our wants and needs to what life provides us. In the meantime, make the most of every day and don't be consumed by worry and anxiety about the future.

Chapter 2

What I Know
(Or At Least Think I Do)

I've been a financial and lifestyle adviser for over 37 years. I've worked with hundreds of wonderful clients and have witnessed many different types of situations over the years. I've also experienced my own ups and downs over the years, including an enriching education at the University of Pennsylvania in Philadelphia; three wonderful children; an unfortunate divorce; an exceptional remarriage; the gift of fabulous grandchildren (God's compensation for getting older); travel around much of the world; a very active life physically with two joint replacements as the result, and now age 60 (or the new 40, as it's being called).

I've also experienced working with some wonderful but perhaps not so fortunate people in my volunteer work over the years—Big Brothers & Sisters, the Boys & Girls Club, and Daybreak, among others. I've met and talked to folks at the lower end of the economic spectrum and people who have been dealt a tough hand in life, and do you know what? Many of these folks are as happy and content as my higher income and higher net worth clients.

What this tells me is that it's not really the amount of income or financial assets you have that's most important, and it's not really what happens to us in our lives that matters most. What's really important is the way we react to our circumstances that matters most. Yes, it's great if we're financially secure or nearly so, and it's great if we've been dealt good fortune. But if not, we can adapt and still be happy and content. And if we've been blessed by good fortune for most of our lives and things change, we can be thankful for the blessings we've received along the way and learn to adjust.

What I know, then, is that it's our attitude that is most important. What goes on between our ears is much more important than what goes on in the rest of our bodies and in the world outside our bodies. I hope you'll agree or at least consider what I'm saying.

Chapter 3

Continuing Widespread Uncertainty in the Financial and Geopolitical Areas

We baby boomers, even though we are a widely diverse group, have many things in common, and perhaps the most important is that we really don't know what to expect from our futures. While I am generally very optimistic, I do have concerns about the future of our country and its role in the global economic and political systems. The significant stock market correction which began in the first quarter of 2000, and from which we are just now recovering, has had a significant impact on the accumulation plans of many baby boomers. It's entirely possible that the growth rates for domestic stocks and equity mutual funds could be in the 5 percent to 7 percent range for the next few years, rather than the traditional 11 to 12 percent long-term rate of return for equities. Coupled with the fact that most baby boomers have not accumulated adequate funds for their financial security, this adds to the uncertainty about our futures.

In addition, the diminished reputation of the United States in worldwide political affairs, for a myriad of reasons, along with the substantial growth of China as well as India and other emerging market countries, questions the financial leadership of the United States in the coming generation. When the significant budget deficits and looming costs of Social Security, Medicare and Medicaid in the future and projected long-term care needs for the baby boomers in their 80s and beyond are taken into account, the future becomes very uncertain for many of us.

Those of us who are seeking to help our children and grandchildren financially see even greater concerns for their futures and will, no doubt, be continuing to help them plan their uncertain futures. For those of us baby boomers who are in the "sandwich generation" the need to help aging parents, along with children and grandchildren, adds to the uncertainty.

I'm not suggesting a high level of pessimism; however, I am cautioning the baby boomer generation that we need to be aware of these uncertainties and be prepared to deal with them if and when they develop. In the meantime, I encourage all of us to stay as positive as possible, to make the most of every day and to balance enjoyment of our present lives with an eye to the risks and uncertainties that may lie ahead of us.

As I mentioned earlier, some of us may be faced with continuing to work or the alternative of downsizing our lifestyle if some of these financial and political concerns are realized. I truly believe that awareness is half the battle.

Chapter 4

The Need to Think About Our Futures

The uncertainty that I addressed in the previous chapter, as well as not really knowing what to expect from our futures, makes it extremely important that we take the time to think about our futures. Most people spend more time planning their summer vacations than they do planning their financial futures. Perhaps it's because it's easy to procrastinate about planning for the future. And perhaps it's because we don't want to face something that doesn't seem to be all that promising for many baby boomers. Our generation has been accused of being the "me generation" and the "now generation", living for the present and not worrying about the future.

I think it is very important to live in the present moment and not dwell on past mistakes and regrets. I also believe it's not good to be overly concerned and worried about the future.

However, while we live in the present moment, we do need to include thoughts about the future, what our future should be over the next three, five and ten years and beyond, and what steps we're willing to take at the present time to make our futures happier and more secure.

After all, life is a series of trade-offs. We can live just for the moment, and as one retired professional baseball player once said, "In looking at my future, I think that if I die next Thursday, I'll probably have enough money to make it to then." Many of us worry about having "too much month at the end of our money", so what's going to happen when we stop working on a regular basis? These are all areas that need to be addressed and evaluated. The more willing we are to plan and set aside funds for the future, without sacrificing too much of our present, the better prepared we will be, whether the future holds brightness and good fortune for us or whether we're forced to deal with some of the potentially looming financial crises, such as Social Security, Medicare and long-term care issues. Spending some time thinking about our futures, then, becomes a very important process for us baby boomers to allocate time to address.

Chapter 5

The Importance of Planning
(More Than Just Our Next Vacations)

The last chapter addressed our need to think about our futures. I'm taking it one step further in this chapter and covering the importance of actually planning our futures and spending more time doing that than planning our next vacations. Thinking about the future is one thing, but developing a visualization and a game plan for what we expect our future to be like in three years, five years, ten years and beyond is really what we need to be doing.

As a Certified Financial Planner, Chartered Financial Consultant and Certified Senior Advisor, I'm in my 38th year of helping people to analyze and plan their futures. I've done an awful lot of planning for my own future as well, balancing current desires with future needs. As a professional in the financial and retirement planning field, I encounter many clients who have just not had the time to do an adequate job of planning. Most of our clients are quite successful financially, as a result of spending more time working for their employers or in their own businesses than on their own financial affairs. Perhaps this is as it should be. However, we all need to spend time thinking about our own financial futures and lifestyles. After all, if we don't do it, who will do it for us?

There are many books that have been written about the importance of planning and many facilities available to assist us in putting together a sound plan for our future. Whether you do it on your own or with the help of a professional—and I naturally strongly encourage using a professional to help you plan your financial future and lifestyle—it is important to devote time to this area. The results can be very significant in terms of improved performance of your financial assets, as well as matching up probable future financial resources with the lifestyle you'd like to enjoy. Even our younger baby boomers, who were born in the 1960s (from 1964 and earlier), can benefit from planning. Your early 40s is not too early a time to start addressing these areas.

Once we reach our 50s (and I know some of us will reach our 60s in 2006), it is very important to start planning seriously for our financial future.

The financial planning process does not take an inordinate amount of time. Initial information can be compiled in several hours, and in three or four sessions of working on your own or with a financial planning professional, you can put together a valuable plan for your future covering various options and contingencies for early retirement, normal retirement, or, more likely for many of us, a redefined retirement involving several phases of cutting back from our current full-time careers to something that gives us a continuing income while enabling us to enjoy life in the future. Trust me, devoting adequate time to this planning area will reap substantial dividends professionally and personally!

Chapter 6

The Importance of Balance in our Lives

So far we've been talking about the uncertainty of the future, and I hope I haven't painted too gloomy a picture of what we might expect down the road. Now I'd like to address an area that is extremely important in dealing with our future but just as important in looking at our present lives. It is so easy in today's society and work environment to get bogged down in day-to-day activities. Some of us have chosen careers or have become involved in careers that demand a great deal of our time and energy. Maybe that's the price of success. For others, it means making sure we take time for ourselves and the truly important things in our lives.

Balance is important, not only in looking at the amount of time and energy we devote to our current goals and pursuits, but also our plans for the future. In looking at current goals and life balance, we should strive to achieve balance among the following areas: personal and family; relationships; health and fitness; career and business; financial; fun time; and contributions, or giving back. In order to have a truly balanced life, we must have goals in all of these areas. Planning our life for today is as important as planning our future.

As a long-time financial advisor, I've seen my practice evolve into what we now call financial life planning. Lifestyle planning and life balance are very important components of the advice we give to clients, and many of our clients have expressed their appreciation for the fact that we look at these broader areas beyond pure financial, retirement and investment planning. Life balance is very important to all of us, and I challenge our readers to spend significant time in these areas.

Chapter 7

Dealing with Uncertainty

We've already talked about change that is going to occur in the future and is already occurring. It's no surprise to any of us that a great deal of uncertainty exists in our world and will continue to. Unfortunately, many people become consumed by worries, fears and anxieties about the future, whether it's what might occur in 15 minutes or 15 years.

Let's face it. Worry is a totally wasted emotion. Studies show that 90 percent of the things we worry about never happen. Life is uncertain, and we need to be adaptable and strong. We should look forward with anticipation to the future no matter what it holds for us. If we have a positive outlook on life, most of the things that we will notice will be positive. If we have a negative outlook on life, most of the things we notice will be negative. So why bother being negative?

Having hope for the future and faith that things have a way of working out for the best for us is the way we should operate. Yes, there are lots of uncertainties, but many of them will produce positive results and will also have some negative results. Life is full of uncertainty. So let's resolve to accept that fact; not worry, hope for a positive outcome; deal with change as it occurs; have a positive expectancy; gratitude for all the good things that happen to us; and a resolve that we can be strong and deal with some of the negatives that life may send our way in the future.

In America especially, we still have a better lifestyle than 90 percent of the world. Let's not worry about what's going to happen with China, Iraq, Israel or North Korea. We can deal with that if and when it comes. In the meantime, let's make the most of every day and resolve to make the world the best we can for ourselves and others and to hope for a positive outcome. Uncertainty is to be expected, but most of what happens to us will be positive.

Chapter 8

Dealing with Change and the Certainty of Change

The last chapter dealt with uncertainty. Change, on the other hand, is something that, although some of us may not like it, is as certain today as the proverbial death and taxes. Change is something we baby boomers have been dealing with most of our lives, and not only the amount of change but the pace of change is expected to increase rapidly.

We need to be adaptable. We need to anticipate change and, hopefully, anticipate it with a positive frame of mind. Changes in our social structure, changes in the dominant position of the United States, which we've been accustomed to; changes in Social Security, pension plans and the way we fund our future financial security; changes in healthcare and long-term care needs; changes in longevity (projections are that three million of us 78 million baby boomers will live to be over 100), etc., etc., are all examples of changes we'll need to deal with.

I guess we can say change is here to stay and we need to be prepared to deal with it. I believe that most of the changes will be for the better and that we in America should expect to continue to enjoy one of the greatest lifestyles and standards of living available in the world. I hope that our political leaders will eventually face these issues and deal with some of the economic and political issues that need to be addressed.

In the meantime, we can be proactive, taking charge of our own lives, expecting change and thinking about how we're going to deal with it. We can expect both positive and negative changes to occur. The positive changes will be easy. The negative will present challenges, which I consider opportunities for growth. One of my favorite expressions is, "Let your challenges be your stepping stones, not your stumbling block". If we expect change and anticipate it, even though we don't know what all of those changes will be, we'll be much better prepared for the futures that lie ahead for us.

Chapter 9

Sixty is the New Forty
(What That Means for Us)

For me, turning age 40 was traumatic; 50 was a non-event, and I'm not so sure yet about 60 as I reach this major milestone. What we are learning is that 60 is no longer old. I've always felt that early middle age begins at 50, so I guess as we baby boomers, especially those of us in our 50s, reach 60 we still have a lot to look forward to. Hopefully, we enjoy good health, a degree of financial security and either careers that are near their peak, are winding down, or perhaps we're already retired. I believe we have a lot to look forward to as we approach 60 and move through middle age. I can remember when I was 18 I thought being 30 years old was ancient. When I turned 40, although it was traumatic, I didn't feel old. Now as I approach 60, I feel pretty much the same way, although with more aches and pains—a replacement hip and knee and somewhat curtailed physical activity.

I feel that life has a lot to offer at this stage of our lives. Perhaps the greatest blessing is watching our children flourish and enjoy the birth and growth of our grandchildren. I think this is especially true among my friends and contemporaries who are starting to enjoy the birth and early youth of their grandchildren. I have many clients in their 50s and early 60s who are sharing the gift of grandchildren, as my wife and I are.

I hope to work till I'm 80, although in a decreasing capacity. Who would have thought when I was 40 that I'd be saying that?

If 50 is early middle age, then I suppose 65 is middle, middle age, and old age doesn't begin until 80. I'm sure I have some older friends who would dispute that 80 is old. I'll let you know when I'm 80 how I feel about it. In the meantime, we should make the most of every day, count our blessings, realize that life has its ups and downs, but to a great degree what we experience in our lives goes on between our ears and our attitude is very important. Our attitude in our 50s and early

60s is very important to our future well being. Make the most of every day and enjoy life.

Chapter 10

Superannuation (or Living Too Long) and What That Means

I tell my friends I'll let them know when I'm 80 how long I want to live. I hope to continue working till 80 and enjoy the lifestyle I've come to expect—a balanced lifestyle, a wonderful marriage, children and grandchildren, lots of time for vacations and relaxation. As I get into my 60s and 70s, I'm hoping that I continue to enjoy good health.

It's interesting that when we're young and have young families, we worry about dying too soon and making sure that our families are provided for. As we reach middle age, one of the biggest fears of baby boomers is living too long. This may mean outliving our financial means and resources. It may mean that Social Security will no longer provide what's been promised to us, or it may mean that healthcare costs and long-term care needs will consume our financial resources. This is a real risk for the baby boomer generation as statistics indicate that 95 percent of baby boomers will not be able to enjoy the lifestyle they've come to expect and that 3 million will live to be over 100. I can't imagine living to be 100. But again, I'll let you know when I'm 80 how much longer I want to live.

Unfortunately, we don't have control directly over how long we're going to live. Yes, we can take good care of ourselves, we can watch what we eat, we can get regular checkups and exercise and, yet, we have no guarantee how long we're going to live. My younger brother developed advanced prostate cancer even though he worked out regularly, watched what he ate, went to doctors for regular checkups, including blood tests and PSA tests. He was told by his primary care physician that his PSA readings were normal. Unfortunately, the primary care physician did not know that even though my brother's PSA readings were low, they were increasing at a regular rate, and that can be a sign of prostate cancer. Fortunately, he has survived the cancer scare, at least at this point. But I know it has had an impact on how he looks at and lives his life.

Rather than worrying about living too long, I think we need to accept it as a risk factor and plan accordingly, but only to some degree. I think it's more important that we live our days mostly for the present moment and take steps to enjoy life while providing a balanced life which incorporates taking care of our children and grandchildren, our spouses and friends, and ourselves. It also means making sure we have provided to some degree for the future, but not while sacrificing everything today. Superannuation is a legitimate concern for some of us, just as dying too soon, being in an automobile or airplane crash, or many of the other surprises that life can deal us. Awareness is half the battle. But we should not live in fear of living too long, just as we should not live in fear of encountering any of life's other negative surprises.

Chapter 11

The Risk of Outliving Our
Financial Resources

The last chapter dealt with the risk of living too long, and a critical component of that is that our financial resources may not last long enough to provide for our financial needs in old age. Most of us who have worked the better part of our careers have come to expect a nominal benefit from Social Security in the form of a lifetime income for our self and our spouse. Unfortunately, a negative cloud hangs over the future of Social Security benefits. I imagine that older baby boomers will receive much or all of their promised Social Security benefits. Benefits have already been reduced in the form of an increasing age for eligibility for full benefits. Younger baby boomers in their 40s probably look at Social Security with greater uncertainty than we older boomers.

Social Security is only intended to provide a basic level of income in retirement. Traditionally, financial advisors and planners talk about the three legs of the stool of financial security, with Social Security being one of the legs. The second leg traditionally has been company-sponsored retirement plans. Unfortunately, over the last 10 to 15 years, there has been a tremendous change in company-provided pension plans. While some companies still provide traditional defined benefit pension plans, with a guaranteed lifetime income, most companies have moved or are moving away from this system. Thus, the ability to provide a guaranteed lifetime income from company-sponsored defined benefit pension plans and from Social Security is less certain.

Many companies, but by no means all employers, provide some form of 401k or profit-sharing benefit, but these plans frequently rely on employee contributions, and they traditionally do not provide a guaranteed lifetime income in retirement unless converted to an annuity. Thus, they are encroaching on the third leg of the financial security stool, which is that of personal savings and investments.

The blending of company-sponsored retirement plans and individual savings in the form of 401k contributions, individual retirement accounts and personal savings and investment strategies has weakened, in my opinion, the financial security hopes of many baby boomers.

Not only are we not saving enough, but we are not taking, nor are we providing, adequate measures to create incomes we can't outlive. This, coupled with increasing life expectancies and the fear of significant long-term care and healthcare costs as we get older and older, has created a major uncertainty in providing for long-term financial security.

One partial solution to this problem is to purchase some form of annuity or annuities to replace traditional pension plans. I am not a big fan of most annuities, especially for people in the current baby boomer generation. However, some form of tax deferred annuity as an accumulation vehicle, with the ability, on an optional basis, to convert the accumulation to some form of guaranteed income in our later years, is a viable option. Generally, I do not encourage clients to annuitize assets until they are at least in their mid- to late-60s, and ideally, not until they are in their 70s or 80s. With increasing life expectancies and relatively low historic interest rates for annuities, immediate annuities are not an attractive solution at the present time. However, the use of annuities as a way of providing additional guaranteed lifetime income is a viable solution to the risk of outliving our financial resources. I am not recommending that all financial assets be annuitized, but only some of them, in some cases, as a way of hedging against living too long and outliving our financial resources.

A final concern is this area relates to increasing healthcare costs and questions whether the government can continue, through Medicare and Medicaid programs, to provide adequate healthcare as our population ages. This, coupled with the higher risk of needing professional long-term care assistance, aside from the medical care issues, constitutes a looming risk of which we baby boomers should be increasingly aware. Whether we can be taken care of in our homes in our advancing years, or whether we require some form of assisted living or nursing home care, the cost of providing this care on top of medical costs, can be overwhelming. Long-term care insurance and supplementary medical coverage can be partial solutions to these risks.

Awareness of these potential risks is of critical importance. Whether we decide to purchase insurance, which can be costly, or whether we decide to partly or fully self-insure the risk, these areas are concerns which we need to address in planning for our financial futures.

Chapter 12

Creating Incomes We Can't Outlive

At the end of the last chapter, I covered the use of annuities as a partial solution to creating incomes we can't outlive. I feel, however, that annuities are only one solution to the challenge of creating lifetime sources of income. Hopefully, Social Security will provide a lifetime income for many baby boomers, especially those of us in our 50s and early 60s. In addition, a good percentage of us have at least some company-sponsored pension programs which provide a lifetime source of guaranteed income (even for companies which have defaulted on their pension obligations, the government provides some guarantees through the Pension Benefit Guarantee Corporation which, hopefully, will remain viable even though it is suffering from multi-billion dollar funding deficits). Utilizing fixed or variable annuities at some point in the future, as I mentioned in the last chapter, can provide some additional sources of lifetime income. Beyond that, with the exception of vehicles such as charitable remainder trusts, private annuities and lifetime non-qualified deferred compensation benefits, not many vehicles exist to provide guaranteed lifetime income.

I feel this is OK if we have set aside enough money to generate ongoing income for the better part of our lives. In addition, many baby boomers will be working well into their 60s and 70s and perhaps even beyond, on a part time or more relaxed basis. This will generate additional assets and income to provide for our futures. A well diversified investment portfolio can provide income which we hope will provide for us for the rest of our lives.

There are no guarantees in life, and we must be willing to take some risks with our retirement income and the risk of living too long. I don't believe that current interest and dividend rates should be counted on to provide cash flow for the rest of our lives. Instead, I believe that a well diversified investment portfolio with a long-term strategy and time horizon can provide cash flow to meet some of our income needs while allowing the overall capital base to continue to grow well into our 70s and 80s and hopefully beyond that if needed. If we have some Social Security benefits and some guaranteed lifetime income from pensions, annuities and similar vehicles, than at least we will have some continuing source of income for life, even if we ultimately run out of our other financial and investment holdings.

Life is full of uncertainty, as I've mentioned previously, and we can only go so far to provide guaranteed income for the long-term future. If need be, we can always adjust our lifestyle at some point in the future as we get older. I know this will not be comforting to some of our readers, but I think that's a reality that many of us may have to face sometime in the future. In the meantime, balancing our lifestyles and our financial needs, both current and future, continues to be a key to some reasonable level of financial security.

Chapter 13

Social Security, Medicare and Long-Term Care Needs—The Financial Time Bombs

Even though I've made reference to these risk areas in previous chapters, I feel that this area is so important that a special chapter should be devoted to covering these areas. Unfortunately, our government leaders have for many years been unwilling to face the huge projected costs of Social Security, Medicare and Medicaid. Either budgetary reductions in other areas or modest tax increases are needed to adequately fund these important programs for our aging society. The government's unwillingness to make these funding commitments, along with a tendency to pass huge budget deficits on to future generations, perhaps even younger baby boomers, but certainly our children and grandchildren, represents fiscal irresponsibility, in my opinion. These time bombs financially are the biggest risk areas we face as we baby boomers get into our 70s, 80s and beyond. This is a real area of concern and yet, I don't believe we can adequately take care of these areas on our own.

The saying, "awareness is half the battle", is especially true when it comes to the future of Social Security and Medicare. Couple these with the need for long-term care assistance for some of us, and we have what could be a real risk factor in our future. So what do we do about it? I think the answer lies in balancing our needs and our wants, putting aside some funds as a hedge to cover these areas, and realizing that life is a series of trade-offs. If we want to enjoy life today, as I think we should to at least some degree, we need to understand that we may have to make adjustments in the future. These financial time bombs of Social Security, Medicare and long-term care needs can be hedged to some degree by us individually; however, I think significant moves by the government will be necessary if we are to enjoy a more secure future.

Chapter 14

Creating or Owning Your Own Business

One of the ways to hedge the uncertainty in our futures is to have our own business, and it's becoming increasingly easy. Having your own business, if you own it, rather than it owning and controlling you, is a great way to generate income in the future and enjoy continuing satisfaction and fulfillment.

Think about the talents you have and the things you might enjoy doing beyond retirement age. And by retirement age, I'm not necessarily talking about age 65. Many baby boomers are being forced to retire well before that age from their traditional jobs. This can be a blessing in disguise as many baby boomers are stressed out or burned out by their career pursuits and no longer enjoy what they are currently doing. Hopefully, we all have talents in areas where we can enjoy ourselves in the future and earn a continuing income if we want or need to.

Starting a business is increasingly easy today, and I suspect it will continue to be so. Also, it doesn't necessarily require a lot of capital. More businesses can be started on the proverbial "shoestring" than ever. And it's increasingly easy to own a business you operate from your own home with little overhead. Whether you have a talent to open a traditional business, a consulting business or an internet-based business, or one of the many legitimate network marketing opportunities that are available today, something should be available to you.

Statistics show that as many as 95 percent of baby boomers will not be able to retire in the traditional sense and enjoy the lifestyles we've come to expect. This may mean significantly curtailing our lifestyles for many of us, just as we have the time and freedom to enjoy retirement-related pursuits. Why not consider starting up a business; or, if you already have one, continuing to operate it on a scaled-back basis? Perhaps that means hiring a support management team, maybe even your succession management plan for the business. On the other hand, it may mean operating your business on a scaled-back basis. Many people in the professions such as medical, dental, legal or financial services, can structure their businesses so that they can work on a scaled-back basis and continue to enjoy much of the income they've earned during their full-time careers. I'm a strong believer in Pareto's Principle, or the 80-20 Rule, which, in this case, indicates that you can earn 80 percent of your income from 20 percent of your effort just by focusing on your most productive and profitable areas.

I challenge you to look at your own situation, what you'd like to be doing in the future, the kind of income you'd like to earn and how you can earn that income while still experiencing, on a part-time basis, all of the joys of being semi-retired, including spending more time with family, grandchildren in particular, traveling and other pursuits that retirees enjoys. I'm convinced that many of us baby boomers can be productive well into our 60s and 70s and even beyond.

Chapter 15

Awareness is Half the Battle

As I mentioned previously in this book, knowing what to expect, awareness of our situation and our future, is half the battle. Many of us operate out of the conventional behavior of ignorance and apathy—that is, we don't know and we don't care. I'm saying this half-jokingly, of course. But unless we decide to focus on the future and take the time to think about what it holds for us, we won't be prepared when surprises come upon us. By taking the time and effort to read this book, hopefully, you are aware of some of the things we can expect as we move into our 60s and 70s. If you are still in your 40s and early 50s, you have time to prepare for the future in a better way than those of us in our late 50s and early 60s.

In any event, much is being written about the future for our generation. There's much scientific literature available.

There are studies funded by the financial services industries, and there are simple fundamentals such as those covered in this book. The more aware we can be of what to expect in the future, the better prepared we'll be for dealing with it. Awareness is truly half the battle.

Chapter 16

Taking Charge

The more proactive we can be in the process of planning for our future, the better off we'll be. An earlier book I wrote several years ago called *Taking Charge: Life-Enhancing Strategies for People Over 40* was designed to address this area in depth. The point I made in the previous book and the point I'm making in this chapter is that we need to be proactive in all aspects of our lives and what areas are more important than those of deciding what our future is going to be? By reading this book, you've been proactive in the process of learning what to expect in your future.

The more we can learn about the demographics of our generation and what the experts are saying, the better off we'll be. However, not all experts are accurate in their predictions. What's really much more important is determining what we want our futures to be like and how best to prepare for them. Being proactive in the process is critically important. Being reactive to what the future may provide may put many of us in no better position than we've been up to this stage of our lives. Many of us have reacted to life's events and circumstances, rather than setting our own course. It's not too late to change the strategy for the next phase of our lives. Decide how you want to live; what kind of life you want; what contributions you'll make; what recreations you'll enjoy; and with whom you want to spend your time in the future. Plan for the future; think about it; set goals and objectives and strategies. These are the keys to achieving the kind of lives we want to have. Good luck in the process.

Chapter 17

Denial and Procrastination

The opposite approach to being proactive and taking charge is to deny that we have a problem, ignore it or, even if we do acknowledge it, to procrastinate in dealing with it. It's good to be optimistic and hopeful for the future, but a dose of realism needs to be stirred into the pot, as well.

I know that in my family, we have a saying that "things always have a way of working out for the best for us", and that seems to be the case with most of our family members and the challenges we face. However, we still need to take steps to prepare for our future and not just live in the present moment all the time.

Our government doesn't seem to be providing a very good example in avoiding the denial posture. Our government has ignored for years and perhaps decades at this point, the looming problems of Social Security and healthcare deficits, which I've covered in earlier chapters. Couple with that the individual responsibility for providing some level of security in our financial futures, and the problem becomes fairly obvious. Most baby boomers don't seem to want to deal with the issue, or at least not deal with it at present. Denial and procrastination are much easier.

I guess that goes hand-in-hand with the charges that the baby boomer generation just lives for today and just lives for ourselves. I don't think this is necessarily true of all of us, and most generalizations, of course, don't apply to everyone. On the other hand, many of us are guilty of this tendency to deny looming challenges in the future and to procrastinate in dealing with them. The sooner we begin to take some steps to hedge the risks in our financial futures, face the facts, take responsibility and deal with them at least in part at present, the better off we will be. In the meantime, I suppose denial and procrastination are not very far removed from their cousins, ignorance and apathy—the "I don't know and I don't care" mentality.

Chapter 18

Stress and Its Cousins:
Worry, Fear and Anxiety

Stress has major impacts on baby boomers, both now and in our futures. Actually, stress is sometimes misunderstood. Certain types of stress, technically referred to as "Eustress", are very beneficial for us. They help us to be motivated, to get up and going, and can be responsible for much of our success and enjoyment in life.

Unfortunately, this is not the type of stress that most people think of. Most people think of stress as a negative, technically known as "Distress". Distress can be the result of many things. It can result from too much good stress; that is, overdoing it. Also, it can result from too much activity without a break for us to refresh and rejuvenate ourselves. Or, it can result from too many negatives bombarding us at the same time.

Negative stress is very common to our American way of life. It directly affects many workers in their 50s as they suffer from burnout or boredom in their careers. This frequently results in a desire to retire early or to do something else. Many times stress is created by forced retirements before we plan to. These downsizings, or capsizings, as they're called, force unintended changes in our lives and frequently a reduction in the level of income we expect to have in retirement. These are all stressful factors.

As far as stress' impact on our future, this is where the cousins of worry, fear and anxiety come into play. If we read articles projecting the future for our generation, we'll read much about the negative consequences of underfunding Social Security and pension plans, too low a savings rate among baby boomers and the impact of healthcare and long-term care costs. These can create stress for many of us and lead to worry, fear or anxiety about our futures.

Worry is a totally wasted emotion. As I mentioned previously, studies show that 90 percent of the things we worry about never happen. Fear, on the other hand, is a concern about a specific event or circumstance, while anxiety is a general feeling of ill being, resulting from unspecified events of circumstances. All three of these emotions of worry, fear and anxiety can lead to additional stress.

The good news is that we can control these emotions by taking charge of our minds and being proactive when it comes to the negative emotions we allow to get into our minds. Stress can be controlled, managed and reduced and so can worry, fear and anxiety. I strongly suggest that we focus our energies on the positives in our lives and work on reducing the negative energies that can affect us. This will prove beneficial in our lives, both now and in the future.

Chapter 19

The Talents of Our Generation

One thing should be clear to all of us baby boomers and those who are younger or older than we: Our generation has contributed much to the present success of the United States. I'm not going to dwell on all of the negatives that have been created by our generation, as well. The purpose of this chapter is to focus on what we have contributed in a positive way and what we still have to contribute. Planning on retiring in our 50s or early 60s can produce a tremendous waste of the use of our talent and experience if we don't put it to good use. As covered previously in this book, many of us will not retire early, but will continue in our careers, or, more likely, find new careers or businesses on a scaled-back basis. Most of us realize that we can't play golf or goof off all the time and that we need to have a healthy channel for our energies and talents.

Whether this is provided through volunteer activities or continuing employment or business ventures, what the baby boomer generation has to contribute to the future of this country and the world is substantial. Yes, we may need to step aside, to a large degree, in the business world to allow the younger generations to take over many of our areas of responsibility. Nonetheless, we have much to continue to offer to the older generation, our generation and the younger generation with our skill and knowledge. I predict that consulting businesses and activities will flourish in our generation and that these consulting efforts will be provided to both for-profit ventures and in the volunteer and non-profit sector. Future generations will be better off as a result of our continuing contributions to society and to business, and we can offer much to our children and grandchildren's generations in providing for future growth, stability and fulfillment in our world. This is perhaps one of our greatest challenges and opportunities. I suggest you look at those areas where your talents can be put to greatest use to help others, as well as ourselves.

Chapter 20

Spirituality (Not Necessarily Religion)

Studies show that many people experience a spiritual reawakening sometime in their 40s, and this continues for many of us into our 50s and beyond. I have always considered myself a fairly spiritual being and, in fact, am a member of an organized religion. However, this chapter is not about religions. A brief comment on religions is in order, however.

Religions seem to provide both good and bad. Many of the wars in history and even today are caused by religious differences. Many atrocities have been committed by religious leaders. The press, of course, loves to cover these negative occurrences. On the other hand, many good things have been accomplished by religions. I don't really want to focus in this chapter on religions, but did want to make those brief comments.

Spirituality is very different from religion and does not require a religious affiliation or involvement. I believe we are both physical and spiritual beings. I believe the universe is made up of both physical and spiritual. In the spiritual realm, there is much that cannot be proven, yet is felt and experienced by many of us.

If, in fact, we tend to become more spiritual as we get older, I think a chapter of this book should be devoted to our spiritual selves. However, baby boomers cannot be characterized or compartmentalized by spirituality. Some of us are highly spiritual beings, while others would deny the existence of spiritual forces and experiences in our lives. There is, as mentioned before, however, a tendency to become more spiritual as we get older.

Whether we believe in a life hereafter, or merely want to provide for something good that extends beyond our lives, does not really matter. For society in general or for our children and grandchildren, spiritual forces play a role in this process.

I encourage readers to take time to consider the role of spirituality in your lives and whether this force has already increased and is expected to increase as you get older. Many contributions to society can be motivated by spiritual forces. I believe strongly in these forces, which have guided me to write this book and the others I have written previously. I believe we are spiritual beings and not just minds and bodies. I encourage all of you to consider this possibility, as well, and evaluate the impact it will have on our future lives.

Chapter 21

Giving Back and Receiving—Tenfold

In 2003, I intended to write a book entitled, *Giving Back: Making Life Better For Ourselves and Our Society*. When I finished writing what I wanted to cover, it turned out to be more like a pamphlet than a book. And yet, I was satisfied that I had covered the important ground. You may have noticed in this book that I have a tendency to cover the basics. Many times they are fundamentals of which we are already aware. But I do not embellish on the subject matter. My philosophy is that you can get to the bottom line quickly, and that's what I hope that people will read and think about. I don't believe in embellishing.

In any event, the subject of giving back is very important, especially when you consider the material I've covered in the last two chapters, covering the talents of our generation and the area of spirituality. I strongly believe that it is important, even essential, that we give back to society the many blessings we have received.

This giving back may take several forms. It may be financially—that is, of our treasure. It may be of our time, talents or thoughts. Whatever it is, it should be something that we enjoy doing and not feel that we are sacrificing. Giving back has its own rewards, and we have much in the way of talent to give to others. And there are many who need our help.

In looking at giving back as an investment, and I suppose this is more of a selfish way of looking at things but acceptable if it takes secondary importance, I strongly believe that we receive back tenfold whatever we give. We may not receive it back directly, and we may not recognize where we have received it unless we look carefully. However, if you stop to think about it, for those of us who have given of our time, talent, treasure and thought, I think most of us will agree that we've received back at least tenfold for what we've given.

Thus, giving back is important in sharing what we know and what we have received with others, but also as a way of making our lives better. I strongly encourage all of you to consider ways that you can give to others and indirectly, look at ways you have already received back a tenfold return on your past giving and sharing efforts.

Chapter 22

Finding Your True Self

In 1996, I wrote my first book, which was also recorded on audio cassette and CD. It was entitled, *Finding Your True Self*, and was a guide to self-awareness and self-actualization. As we baby boomers move into the more mature stages of our lives, I think it is very important for us to learn more about ourselves, finding out who we are, being aware of our surroundings and trying to make the most of the gifts that we have received. The concept of *Finding Your True Self* is one that's very familiar to many baby boomers. Hand-in-hand with the increased awareness of spirituality as we get into our 40s and beyond is the concept of spending more time finding out who we truly are.

Unfortunately, some of us have not yet begun to face these questions. I feel it is very important in making the most of the rest of our lives, both from a selfish standpoint and from the standpoint of sharing with others, that we know who we are. Finding our true selves is an important part of determining our future as baby boomers. Some of you might be interested in reading or listening to a copy of *Finding Your True Self: A Guide for Self-Awareness and Self-Actualization.*

Chapter 23

Enjoying Yourself Now—the Trade-offs

Baby Boomers have frequently been accused of being the "me" generation and just living for the present. There is something to be said for living in the present moment, especially if you read Eastern philosophies. Fearing the future and dwelling on negatives that have occurred in the past can be very harmful to us in the long run. However, just living for today and not worrying about what the future holds is irresponsible.

Once again, the concept of balance in our lives is the key. I would never suggest that we sacrifice too much of our present lifestyle and enjoyment for the future. On the other hand, it is necessary to do proper financial and retirement planning and to be putting aside some money for the future. A minimum of 10 percent of our income is a good rule of thumb.

But for many of us, 20 to 30 percent is more appropriate, as long as we still have means to provide for our present enjoyment. I know this is tough for many of us who are still helping to get children through college and, perhaps, caring for elderly parents at the same time.

The generation of our parents, after World War II for we older baby boomers, was known for sacrificing everything to provide for us. And I think most of us are very grateful for the sacrifices of that generation and the opportunities they afforded us. Those sacrifices are less common in the baby boomer generation, and many of us are living too much for today and will probably regret it sometime in the future.

Again, I think it's important to balance current needs and desires with some responsible level of financial planning, saving and investing for the future. With the uncertainty of Social Security, Medicare and long-term care issues, and the decline in company-sponsored pension plans, we need to take greater responsibility for achieving some level of financial independence in the future. If we aren't willing to do that, then we need to be aware of the potential consequences and the fact that we may have to alter our standard of living at some point in the future. As I've covered before, working at least in some reduced capacity beyond normal retirement age may be a partial solution for many of us.

Chapter 24

Summing It Up—Planning Your Future and Living It

I hope I've given our readers at least some worthwhile suggestions that will have an impact on our future and what we can expect. Thinking about and planning for our future is far more important than planning our next vacation. Yet, many baby boomers do not want to face the issues of what our futures will be like.

I think our futures can be very bright if we take some steps to provide for a relatively secure future. We can balance our present enjoyment and lifestyles with adequate plans for the future. The most important thing is to live your life in the present moment, make the most of every day and enjoy your friends and family members and what this wonderful country has to offer. Enjoy today while making some provisions for the future.

I wish you all the best of luck in achieving your goals for the present and the future!

Printed in the United States
61754LVS00005B/133-183